A Journey Out of Darkness

For a Grieving Heart

Joanne Holbrook

A Journey Out of Darkness

by Joanne Holbrook

Copyright © 2021 Joanne Holbrook

ISBN: 9798590562749

Published by Amazon KDP

All rights reserved. No part of this book may be reproduced, distributed, or transmitted in any form or by any means, including electronic, mechanical, photocopying, recording, or by any information storage and retrieval system without permission in writing from the author

Foreward

I remember very clearly the day I first met Joanne. She came to the church (Christ Fellowship Church in Dawsonville, Georgia) where I am on staff and where we both attend. Someone had told me, "There is a woman waiting for you in the lobby. She wants to buy one of Pastor Todd's books." I hurried off to meet her and then walked with her to our book table.

We sat down at the table and she began to search for her checkbook. As she shuffled through her purse, she began to tell me her story and tears began to flow from her beautiful brown eyes. She had lost her daughter only a short time ago and I could tell her heart had been crushed beyond imagination. I held it together as best I could, but on the inside I was crumbling to my knees. I thought, "How in the world can this precious lady live each day with such heart-wrenching loss?!" I am a mother of two wonderful young men and I simply could not imagine! It took all I had to refrain from saying, "Stop! I cannot listen any more!"

Then all of a sudden, her story took a drastic turn. She began to share about an encounter she experienced with Jesus one day while crying out to Him over a particular situation (you will read about it in chapter 5!). The Lord came to her in a powerful way as she read Psalm 91 and she realized Jesus was her

Defender! She was immediately filled with the Holy Spirit as she fully surrendered her life, her hopes, her grief, and her future to Him! We rejoiced together right there at the book table over the goodness (So good!) of God and how faithful He is, even in times we feel like we are completely falling apart.

Because of Jesus and His faithfulness and goodness to Joanne, she has written this book so others may be healed. Everyone faces trying times, challenges, loss, and at times even tragedy. We ask the tough questions like, "Will I make it through this?" "Can I move on?" "Will the pain ever go away?" And yes even, "Where is God?" Joanne's story brings us the answer to all these questions, Jesus. Just Jesus.

I appreciate her willingness to open her heart and share how the Lord has walked with her through the most unbelievable pain and loss anyone could experience. I am certain it was difficult beyond measure to relive the events surrounding the death of her precious daughter in order to write this book. Her aim in sharing her story is that others will find Jesus in the same way she did and surrender their broken heart to Him that He may bring healing and wholeness to their soul.

Thank you, Joanne, for being willing to lay your heart before us and share your story. May everyone who reads this book realize the power and faithfulness of Jesus no matter what tomorrow may bring. I know this is the intent of your heart, to glorify Him and bring others *into the wonder of Who He truly is!*

Karen Smith
President, KINEO Ministry Training Center
Christ Fellowship Church
Dawsonville, GA

Dedication

With much love, I am dedicating this book to the memory of Emily Paige Holbrook. She was my youngest daughter and took her life at the young age of 32. Her two daughters, Ryleigh Grayson Threet and Sadie Lane Hansard, now ages 14 and 12, have adjusted to a daily life without each other and a life without their mother. I also want to dedicate this writing to them because I know they are going to do, in double, what their mother did not finish here on earth. I lift Ryleigh and Sadie up to the throne room of Heaven and intercede on their behalf. Deposits are being made! Watch out satan (no mistake with the small *s*), these two girls are up next!

Acknowledgements

My Husband

Andy, I want to thank you for hanging in there with me through the bad and the ugly, and through the darkest hours of our lives. Many marriages end in divorce after the death of a child, and I thank God that we survived the storm together. Our love and the grace of God has held us together!

It is also because of you that I am painting on stage Sunday nights at the *North Georgia Revival*. You spend many hours every week building my wood canvases and setting up the stage to make it happen. I could not do it without you. We are a team!

Pastors Todd and Karen Smith

Thank you both for leading me to the next level of spiritual growth and for supporting me while I fulfill my purpose to paint in the Spirit. You have been faithful in hosting God's presence in one of the most amazing revivals in history, and I stand in awe that I am alive to be a part of it. Through your "full gospel" teachings, and the Kineo Ministry Center, God is building an army that He can use for the end days. I love you both and cannot imagine partnering anywhere else other than *Christ Fellowship Church*.

Family and Friends

I want to thank all my family and friends for standing by my side while walking through this journey. There were days and nights of endless tears that you endured with me. I know that many of you wondered if the person you once knew would ever return. You were there when I cried out to Jesus, and you watched me cling to Him for survival. Thank you for your prayers and never giving up on me!

Thank you, from the bottom of my heart, for helping me with this book. It took a tribe to put it together, but we made it! Through all of you, the Lord provided all the skills and talents needed for the preparation and editing needed for publication.

Introduction

On May 18, 2015, life for me changed forever. It was on that day I received the phone call every mother fears most. My husband, Andy, called to tell me I needed to leave work immediately and come to Emily's house. Emily was our youngest daughter. She was a single mom with two little girls and struggled with life's challenges. Upon arrival, Andy told me…"She's gone!"

I am alive today because I cried out to Jesus. Having only the faith for going to Heaven, I was not prepared for this journey. I never journaled a day in my life, nor read many books prior to Emily's death, but I quickly heard a prompting in my spirit to read the Bible. It was there that the Lord met me, comforted me, taught me, and provided the strength to carry me through this grief journey. He never left me!

It is my heart's desire for other grieving hearts to cry out to Jesus. This writing is the story of my journey with Jesus, my journal entries, Emily's life and death, and my testimony. Yes, I have a testimony! The enemy thought he would seek out our entire family, and the next victim was me. He has been caught, and bound, in Jesus' name!

Table of Contents

Foreward by Karen Smith..3

Dedication...6

Acknowledgements..7

Introduction..9

Chapter 1: In the Eye of the Storm.............................11

Chapter 2: Looking Back..19

Chapter 3: Emily..37

Chapter 4: Stepping into the Light..............................45

Chapter 5: Psalm 91...57

Chapter 6: New Beginnings..63

Chapter 7: I Have Overcome......................................81

Chapter One

In the Eye of The Storm

It is December 2, 2015, and I awaken early to the sound of rain pelting down on my bedroom windows. It is dark, gloomy, and the wind is howling. I cannot describe my mood any better! As I fight back the tears, I count the number of months it has been since my daughter's death. Only six months. That means, I have about eighteen months left if I fall into the average time it takes for a grieving soul to heal. That is what *we* do…*we*, as in those who are grieving. We count the days, hoping and praying that the pain will soon subside.

As I lie here fighting the desire to go back to sleep, I fix my eyes on Emily's picture with her two daughters. I shake my head in disbelief. This is not fair! It is not natural! I am supposed to die before my children! At age 32, her death was tragic and

unexpected. Suicide! Taking her own life! This is the news you hear in the media; it happens to other people! People die every day from freak accidents, car accidents, and plane crashes; at least you can explain those deaths, even though they too, are tragic and unexpected. Lord, give me something I can understand; something I can explain!

Emily's daughters, Ryleigh and Sadie, were her life. She was a single mother, and I watched her struggle under the weight of life's pressures and demands. She sacrificed her personal needs; her girls came first. With every decision, remarks were made about how it would affect the girls' wellbeing. I loved seeing her as a mother instead of a daughter; her selflessness was inspiring. I often told her, "You're a much better mother than I was, I would be cleaning the house!" Rather than seeking a career, she chose a simple life. I see her now as I look back, whether it be on the floor playing together, or teaching them the alphabet and numbers in the bathtub with sponge toys, she was fully present in the moment. Looking at her picture, I remember what I read recently about how important it is to think about the good times, the good memories, and not her death.

Emily was beautiful, both inside and out. She had dark brown eyes, and long, dark brown hair that was very shiny. No one in our family had hair like that. When she rocked her babies, they would wrap their hands around her hair until they fell asleep. Emily's grandfather, *"DaDa,"* referred to her as his *little brown eyed Indian girl* when she was young. These genetic features came from her great grandmother who was a Cherokee Indian descendant.

Ryleigh and Sadie have different fathers, so immediately following Emily's death they were now separated from one another, from me, and from the daily life that they knew and loved. I call this tragedy my loss times three.

#1 - I am grieving the loss of my daughter.

#2 - I am grieving the lost time I spent with Ryleigh and Sadie.

#3 - I am grieving for their loss of sistership, pain, and suffering.

Grieving is extremely painful and misunderstood by those who know and love you. It is a journey that takes you places you never imagined. For me, the worst is the physical pain such as fatigue, loss of appetite, headaches from endless crying, jaw pain from clinching my teeth at night, and the continuous gut-wrenching pain in my stomach. In addition to my physical pain there are emotional and mental dimensions I am dealing with such as anger, denial, guilt, isolation, rejection, confusion, and forgetfulness. Things I used to do without effort are now a huge chore. Even simple things like taking a shower, or preparing my breakfast, are now difficult. I have been in a fog for several months and feel like I am outside of my body looking in from a distance. There are strange feelings that make me wonder if I am going crazy.

Being around my eldest daughter, Jessica, and her two children, Olivia (age 7) and Brooks (age 4), take me back to Emily's death and the separation of her children from one another. There is happiness with Jessica and her family, and complete brokenness from Emily's tragic death. I cannot separate the two. Emily's death suddenly dissolved her family. The home she rented was quickly emptied of all her belongs, and those of Ryleigh and Sadie. They are now living with their fathers in different cities. No more laughter together, no more laughter with their mommy, no more playing together in their rooms. For many weeks, maybe months, I have been alienating myself from Jessica and her family. She is hurting and does not understand this emotion. How can I hurt my only living daughter like this; what is wrong with me?

One thing you can surely expect when grieving is a grief ambush. The word ambush means surprise attack. I never know when or where this will happen. At a grocery store, I round the corner and see a young woman with the same color hair and size as my daughter, with two small children. My tears are now uncontrollable! The attack is so strong and sudden, I leave without getting what I went to buy. At that moment, the item was not important. Another grief ambush happened when a few friends came over to visit. We are outside grilling, when suddenly I realized that a mother and her children are in our pool having fun together. That was Emily's favorite place with her girls! I wanted them out of the pool! I was angry and ran into the house so no one would notice my outburst of tears.

After a few sessions of counseling, I learn that I am not crazy and that everyone's grief journey is unique. There is no right or wrong way to grieve. Reading as many books as possible, written by people who have personally experienced grief from the death of a loved one, is a source I am using to find peace. I am not desiring the age-old saying that *misery loves company*, instead I am searching for someone with whom I can relate. How are others coping?

Relationships with my family and friends are now affected because no one knows what to say, or how to comfort me. My husband, Andy, and I are grieving differently, so naturally we encounter conflicts with one another. He does not understand my needs, or how I feel. I can't explain it to him because I do not understand myself what is happening to me. He, on the other hand, needs me and I do not know how to help him or comfort him. It is obvious that my friends are at a loss for words. They want to help me but are afraid they will say or do the wrong thing. Some avoid me, some cry with me, and some just say all the wrong things. No one is given a manual on how to care for a friend who is grieving.

It has only been a few months since Emily's death, and there are moments that I want to die so I can be in Heaven with her. I say to my family, "I just want to go home," and I am not talking about my earthly home. This is not an option because my family needs me, my grandchildren need me, and God has a different plan for me. I do not want to take my life, but I do not want to live in my current situation either. I am trapped in what feels like a time warp.

"I am in the eye of a storm!"

A prayer for you…

"Father, I know there are many grieving over the loss of a loved one; I know the depths of their pain! Oh Lord, where would I be right now if I had not cried out to You! I pray their hearts will turn to You, the only One who can heal and restore! Father, I do not have to beg you to meet them where they are because You have already promised that you will never leave them or forsake them! May they feel Your presence now, Lord Jesus! May they feel Your arms around them! In Jesus' name, A-men!

Scriptures: Joshua 1:9, Deuteronomy 31:8, 1 Kings 8:57, Genesis 28:15, 1 Chronicles 28:20, 1 Peter 5:7, Jeremiah 29:11, Psalm 55:22

Chapter Two

Looking Back

I was raised by a single mother who worked very hard to keep a roof over our heads and food on the table. Daddy was an abusive alcoholic, and Momma eventually divorced him after many years of praying for a miracle. I am the eldest of three living siblings (one brother, one sister). Their first child, Regina, died at the age of five with leukemia when I was nine months old. There was one single portrait of her in our home, taken before her illness took a turn for the worse. She was sitting very proudly on a table with her hands crossed in her lap, wearing a beautiful red dress. Momma rarely spoke of Regina. When I wanted to know more about her, I would ask Granny and Papa. They would tell me all about her illness and how there was no cure in those days for leukemia. In looking at old photos of

Momma and Daddy holding Regina when she was sick, I could see the pain and suffering on their faces (undoubtedly, the reason Daddy turned to alcohol).

Looking back on my childhood is painful. Growing up with an alcoholic father determined the outcome of each day --- would it be a happy day or a fearful day? When Daddy was not drinking, he was humble, kind, and down-right funny at times. He often referred to me as *Raquel Welch* because of my brunette hair, and my sister, Karen, was called *Marilyn Monroe* because she was our blonde beauty! I hold on to those remarks because it was his way of telling us we were beautiful…his highest and best compliment!

My brother, Neal, was born when I was twelve. He was a surprise, the last child in our family, and the last and only grandson on Daddy's side of the family. Daddy was one of four siblings, and they all had girls! Ten girls, until Neal came along! Everyone in our extended family was overwhelmed with joy over this baby boy! We honestly did not know what to do with him! A boy?!?!

Daddy remained sober for a long time after Neal was born…could this be our miracle? Neal was his life! I am sure I would have been jealous if I'd had a normal loving relationship with Daddy, but I was so excited for this chance of a miracle it didn't matter to me that he was so in love with this little boy. A son!

Over time, Daddy started drinking again. A mixture of alcohol and pills turned him into a completely different person. Instead of laughing at him, I would be terrified of him. I hated to see Fridays come when he was holding down a job because it was typically payday. He had money in his pocket, and money to stay out with other men and drink for days on end, or until the money ran out. I would start asking Momma on Friday afternoons if it was time for Daddy to be home. If he did not arrive on time, fear would set in. It was time to buckle down!

Momma was a beautiful, kind, quiet, small woman. Though small in stature, she was a giant in strength. It was Momma that raised us, while Daddy was in and out of rehab, jail, or prison. It always required at least two jobs, and being the oldest child left me feeling an enormous amount of responsibility to help her financially. Going around the community and offering my services to baby sit was the first opportunity to make my own money. Growing up quickly (little time for fun and games) was a must.

The community we lived in at that time was small. A community where *everyone knew everyone*, and most attended the local Baptist church. I attended this church from the time I was born, until I moved away when married. At the age of nine, I accepted Jesus as my Lord and Savior. Attending Sunday school and singing in the choir were all part of my regular routine.

As life rolled on, I stayed in church with Andy and our two daughters. We raised our girls in the 80's...big hair, ugly clothes, and high interest rates! We managed to drag ourselves into church after rushing around trying to get dressed, eat breakfast, and find our Bibles. Arguing about something on the way, and almost losing our religion before entering the church, was to be expected almost every Sunday. I prayed the prayers, sang the songs, asked for my sins to be forgiven, and started my normal week on Monday. My Bible would be put somewhere afterwards, but never read; maybe praying if there was a need. It was all about me – me – me... my children, my life, my marriage.

Secret Things

Momma died on July 12, 1988, at the age of 49 of breast cancer. During her funeral service, one of the ministers talked about a wonderful visit he had with her in the hospital. He said that she quoted Deuteronomy 29:29...*Secret things belong to the Lord*. I could never remember a time in my life when my momma quoted scripture, so I was happy to learn she found comfort in this scripture during her illness. I never thought about it again.

It was a beautiful, sunny, Sunday morning on September 18, 2015. I know the date because it is written in my journal!

Instead of going to church, I felt the need to have quiet time at home with God. I took my Bible and journal outside and let the sun shine down on me. I prayed, I cried, and I sang with the music I had playing on the outdoor speakers. I lifted my hands toward Heaven, and I allowed Jesus to fill me with His love. I filled up six pages in my journal as words began to pour out of me! The pages are stained from my tears. God instantly sent me Deuteronomy 29:29...*Secret things belong to the Lord.* I can't even begin to explain the feeling I had. My mind raced back to my mother's service. I could feel God's presence, and although I do not fully understand the connection to this scripture, I rest in knowing that more things will be revealed to me in due season.

Why Can't I Pray?

About a year before Emily's death, I began slipping away from God totally. My focus was on Emily and her children. Becoming so engulfed in her life, there was no room for God. She became my idol! Going to church had ceased, and so had praying. There were many times I could not find my Bible.

One afternoon, on a drive home from work, a strange feeling came over me. I thought about God and where I stood with Him. Feelings of condemnation, shame and fear overpowered me. Turning down the volume on the radio, I tried to make sense of it all. I tried to pray…but could not. Weeks later this happened again, and in the same place…my car. This time, it was almost like a voice or a tap on the shoulder. I asked, "God, what is wrong with me…what is happening to me?" I tried to pray, but again without success. "Dear God,"…then nothing. I was terrified! Why can't I pray?

Months later, I am soaking in my garden tub, a place where I could get away. Out of nowhere, an old Baptist song I used to sing when I was young popped into my head… *There's Just Something About That Name.* I began to sing what I could remember… "Jesus, Jesus, Jesus, there's just something about that name…Master, Savior, Jesus, like the fragrance after the rain." As I sang these words I began to cry. I knew something was wrong, and I needed Jesus in my life…yet He seemed so far away.

It happens again! In my car, the same prompting from the Lord! Still struggling to pray, I remembered the song *There's Just Something About That Name,* then began calling out His name… "Jesus!" "Jesus, please don't forget me!" "Jesus, hold me!" I felt like something horrible was going to happen. I was convinced God was telling me a storm was coming my way and I would need Him. I knew I was going to experience some sort of pain. Would someone die? Would it be Andy? Coming home from work one afternoon, I found the refrigerator door standing open. "Andy!," I yelled! My heart was pounding, and the worst case of fear swelled over me! Until he walked in, I thought he was dead. My fear subsided, but there was still an uneasiness I was battling within that I had not shared with anyone.

The Red Cardinal

The storm that I felt was coming began on Monday, May 18, 2015. That morning, I had my usual 8:30 am sales meeting. I wheeled into the parking lot while talking on the phone with Emily. She told me how excited she was to be meeting with someone to help her with a personal matter that afternoon. She said she had just dropped the kids off at school and was planning to put a roast in the crockpot...her favorite! I told her I loved her, and we ended our conversation.

After the meeting, I hurried out to my sales office to begin my day. At this time, I was a real estate agent and sold new homes for a local builder in Atlanta. My desk was in front of a large window that overlooked a beautiful landscape. I noticed that a cardinal flew right up to my window and landed on the limb of a crepe myrtle. It flew away almost as quickly as it landed, a *blink of an eye* moment. I remember saying..."Wow, what a beautiful bird!" His color was brilliant red! Then it occurred to me that I had never seen this bird here before.

Weeks later, I read that red cardinals are believed to be spiritual messengers connecting Earth and Heaven. In this article, it stated that the word cardinal is derived from the Latin word "cardo," which means hinge. Much like a door hinge, the cardinal is represented as an entryway between earth and spirit. They carry the message in and out, to and fro. "Is there something to this," I asked? Was the bird delivering a message? Was it a symbol of Emily's spirit since it appeared around the time of her death? The article continued to say that red cardinals are symbolized as the living blood of Jesus Christ. In the Christian context, the blood of Jesus and cardinals are both used as the symbols of everlasting vitality. Scripture clearly says, "By His blood, we are freed from sin to serve the living God, to glorify Him, and to enjoy Him forever." A red cardinal represents life, hope, and restoration. I never saw the cardinal again, but what amazed me even more was to learn that they live in the same area, so why hadn't I noticed him before now? I had been gazing out that window for almost three years at that point.

I Cried Out

Moments after the cardinal incident, around 11:00 AM, I received a phone call from Andy telling me that something was wrong at Emily's house and to get over there as quickly as possible. Upon arrival, I saw crime scene tape around her house, and the street was filled with multiple police cars, firetrucks, and an ambulance. I rushed over to Andy. He said…"She's gone!"

There will never be two words more life changing than those. My mouth became bone dry, my body shook, and the world started spinning. I was out of control with pain! I had two choices at that moment – I could shake my fist at God, or I could cry out for Him. **I CRIED OUT**! Standing in the driveway, I stretched out my arms and hands as far as I could, and shouted…"Jesus," "Jesus,"…"I need you"…"I can't do this without you!" I remember looking at the sky and the clouds. I remember seeing the tops of green trees, and the birds singing. It was a beautiful spring morning. I cried and shouted out for Jesus while looking at the blue sky and clouds for what felt like an eternity. I could actually feel my daughter's spirit, as she had just passed through the same sky I was now looking at. Life for me had stopped, but I knew that the world was still alive. I was upset that I could hear birds singing and cars driving by. How dare life and happiness continue at a moment like this! Falling to the ground, I continued to shout for Jesus. I screamed His name until my voice became so raspy that no one could understand me. "Oh, Lord Jesus, I know she belongs to You," I shouted! "How can I do this, Lord?" "No, No, No, it can't be, Lord," I cried out! "What will Ryleigh and Sadie do, they need their mommy, Lord!" "Jesus, Jesus, help me," I shouted! I was aware of my surroundings, yet could not comprehend what was happening. In my agony, my body was being split in the middle...a world that continued, and a world that ended. The pain was so severe, it felt as if I were being gutted like an animal, and the organs of my body were spilling out onto the pavement!

I made it through the first night. One down, and thousands more to go. Andy and I slept arm in arm and cried until we fell asleep. Emily, our baby girl, was gone! In an instant! Unable to comprehend it then, I slept through without medication. Undoubtedly, this was the Lord's loving arms around me! I needed to be with Ryleigh and Sadie, but they were now with their fathers. It was all too much, too hard, too painful. In my mind, I would not survive this loss!

Day 2: I'm in a fog with darkness all around. Was this a bad dream? How do I get out of bed and face this day!? Our pastor from church, Shawn Lovejoy, came to console us and discuss arrangements for Emily's service. As he heard my story and watched the tears stream down my face, he leaned over and said, "Do you know how BIG your God is?" That question hit me like a bolt of lightning.

> *For the word of God is living and powerful, and sharper than any two-edged sword, piercing even to the division of soul and spirit, and of joints and marrow, and is a*

> *discerner of the thoughts and intents of the heart.*
> Hebrews 4:12 (NKJV)

God was speaking to me, through Pastor Shawn. He then said, "He's got this!" From that moment on, I knew God was with me and He would never forsake me! That was God's grace, for He heard my cries on the day of Emily's death! If I had any hope of surviving this pain, this loss, this grief, I knew I needed God in my life in a deeper way.

In the weeks following, being showered with devotionals, books, and literature on grief, I put them beside my bed and thought I would get to them later...maybe when I felt better. How could I possibly receive comfort from any of these books? Shortly afterward, I received a package from a friend. It contained two books...*Grief Share-A Journey from Mourning to Joy*, and *Psalms, for the Grieving Heart*. She also included a journal for writing. There was a sweet note inside the package. She told me about tragically losing her son five years ago, and how this material ministered to her. She encouraged me to write in the journal, even if I had little to say. She said it was a very powerful tool in her healing. I instantly felt a connection because of our similar losses. I told myself I would read the devotionals, but I was not sure about journaling.

I have never been one to read very much, and certainly never kept a diary or journaled. I began reading the Psalms devotional. My Bible was there beside my bed, so I dusted it off and used it to look up the scriptures. Day one was from Psalm 31. It grabbed my attention quickly because it was about King David *crying out to the Lord* during a time of adversity. Oh, my goodness, I thought! I already knew that God used our pastor to reveal to me just how BIG God is. Now, I realized that the lady who mailed me this package was also an instrument of God. I must read everything; God has something for me!

For the first time, I read the Bible with a different set of eyes. I pondered it, longing for God to meet me there. I was aching for comfort, peace, and answers. After the Psalm reading, I turned to the Grief Share book. The first reading was *Understanding Your Grief*. There was a prayer at the end...

> "Lord God, teach me to embrace my grief and not fight it, so that I may experience the true healing that comes from You. Amen".

I reached for my journal and made my first entry dated June 7, 2015. As I stated before, I had never journaled. I only quoted what spoke to me from both readings...

"Cry out to the Lord, you will be heard! My groans feel merciless at times, I can't silence them. God knows every inch of my grieving heart. Nothing remains hidden from Him."

I cannot explain it, but strength was found in writing these words down. They were not my own, but they spoke to me and that was all I could do at the time. There was peace beginning to settle in my soul. God's Word was quickening my spirit, and I could feel an intimacy with Him like never before.

Stepping into The Word

As I continued reading, I would feel God's presence and peace. I have read that people who are grieving find that nights are the worst. It is a time when things are dark and uncertain. For me, it was the best time because it was when I met God and allowed Him to speak to me. I fell asleep each night drenched in His Word. I felt His arms around me. Did this stop the pain, the tears, the grief? NO!

Mornings would bring fear, and they continued to come. I would wake up around 4:00 am with a painful ache deep within my stomach. That was my *gut-wrenching* pain. The room would be dark, and fear would set in. I had been reading that fear is not of God, and to immediately turn to Jesus for comfort and direction. I would cry out in the middle of the night..."Jesus, Jesus!" On most occasions, I would fall back to sleep and morning eventually came. I would still wake up with this pain, but now I must get out of bed and put one foot in front of the other and face the day.

I am still grieving as of this writing. The good news I want to share with you is that God has been right there with me on this grief journey, and He will be with you also if you allow space in your heart for Him! He does not stop my grieving, but I know that He is here by my side and He will sustain me. He has a record of every tear I've shed...

> *You number my wanderings; put my tears into Your bottle; are they not in Your book? Psalm 56:8 (NKJV)*

Now, that is a BIG God wouldn't you say? I also cling to His promise written in John 16...

> *Most assuredly, I say to you that you will weep and lament, but the world will rejoice; and you will be sorrowful, but your sorrow will be turned into joy. John 16:20 (NKJV)*

God has enabled me to see a bigger picture. Emily's death will not be wasted. I do not know by what, or how, but I know God will use my testimony for His purpose, in His time.

Our time here on earth is like a vapor in God's eyes (James 4:14). When He comes again, everything will be revealed to us. We will see how God used our pain and suffering for His eternal purpose. In the meantime, I envision a huge puzzle that God is putting together to fulfill His plan. It is coming together piece by piece, but I still cannot see the full image. When Emily died, there was a puzzle piece that represented her life and God put it into place. It adds a little more detail, a bit more color, and helps to close in the gap. No other piece will fit in that spot, and the puzzle cannot be complete without it.

Jesus Carried Me

At an early age, I had a strong desire to draw and paint. I would save my babysitting money to buy sketchpads, paint, and canvases. I never considered myself an artist because I looked at a photo or picture for inspiration; this felt like cheating to me since it was never an original.

Since Emily's death, I have felt the rest and peace of Jesus while He is carrying me through this storm. With that came a vision that I knew I had to paint. This all seemed strange because I had not painted in many years. As I painted Jesus carrying me through the darkness, I began to paint bright streaks of white covering up the darkness. It was not what I saw in my vision at all, as I only saw the darkness. I almost tossed the painting, thinking that I blew it. I believe this painting will be used in the future and has a greater meaning than I realize…

A prayer for you…

"Lord God, please comfort the person reading this right now! Comfort them in their mourning. Give them the desire to read Your Word, and make it come "alive" for them as it did for me. Meet them there! Place them under your wings and give them rest, Lord! Oh, how I remember asking for rest in the beginning days! Thank you in advance, Lord, for providing their every need. In Jesus name, Amen."

Scriptures: Matthew 11:28-30, Exodus 33:14, Psalm 23, John 16:33, Philippians 4:6-7

Chapter Three

Emily

Beautiful, meek, humble, simple, quiet, transparent, selfless, and shy are just a few of the words describing Emily. As a child, she was easy to please, and loved pleasing others. Her love for cleaning and organizing at a very young age fascinated us. Members of our extended family would often ask Emily to come clean rooms or closets. She could not wait to tell us all about "the before and after," and all the improvements she made!

Emily loved and admired her older sister, Jessica. The house we lived in while they were growing up was within walking distance to their grandparents (Mamo and Dada) and cousins. It was not uncommon for them to walk to Mamo and Dada's house and stay most of the day. Mamo was a wonderful cook, so most visits consisted of eating a meal or two before they returned home. Family gatherings during birthdays and holidays were also special to Emily...she loved giving handmade cards and gifts!

Another favorite was the annual camp meeting revival at *Holbrook Campground.* For ten days, in the middle of the summer in GEORGIA, we moved into a one room cabin - called a tent - with no air-conditioning and pine shavings covering the dirt floor. Emily looked forward to this event as much as she did Christmas. We shared this tent with multiple family members in the Holbrook clan! Nice and cozy! When church services were not being held underneath the arbor, the kids would ride their bikes, throw water balloons, and eat watermelon on the back porch. There were almost 100 cabins built around the arbor, in a circular fashion, and all children were taken care of and monitored as they freely ran from one to another. In our tent, bunk beds lined the walls with no privacy! It was like a scene from *The Waltons* (TV show). At night we would repeat the famous..."good night, John Boy...good night Mary Ellen!" Most of the family did not care where they slept, but Emily had her own designated place each year, and everyone knew it! She spent weeks prior to opening day spiffing up and decorating her area. Accepting Christ as her savior, on her bunk bed one night after service, made this place even more special.

As a young adult, Emily began to experience an occasional episode of depression. Later in her life, there seemed to be more onsets that eventually led to oppression. Depression is a mood disorder that causes a persistent feeling of sadness and loss of interest. It affects how one feels and behaves and can lead to a variety of emotional and physical problems. The definition of oppression is the unfair or cruel use of power to control another. What, or who, was using cruel power to control Emily? Since the Word tells us we do not fight flesh and blood, but against principalities, against powers, against the rulers of the darkness of this age, against spiritual hosts of wickedness in the heavenly places (Ephesians 6:12), then the answer is satan. So how did satan oppress Emily? The answer best given is condemnation.

Like most of us, Emily made poor choices that later led to consequences she suffered. The one poor choice that perpetuated life-long pain was having an abortion. How could you air her dirty laundry, you might ask? If the purpose of this book is to minister, help the grieving, and speak to someone who is seeking help, then it needs to be written. I know in my heart this is what Emily would want. During the brief period that we spoke about the abortion, she told me that she wanted to volunteer at a local pregnancy crisis center. She even visited once and spent some time there, but nothing ever transpired. If she could speak to me right now, she would say…"Mom, please tell the world, let my story be told and heard, help others!"

I did not know about the abortion when it happened. She was 16 years old and suffered through it without family. Years later, at 25 years old and during a difficult time, Emily approached me and said she needed to tell me something. We sat down, looking eye to eye. It was obvious this was going to be a serious conversation. She began by apologizing, as if she had done something horrible to me personally. The tears began to flow, the trembling set in, and full-blown fear consumed her. Before she said any more, I tried to settle her by saying, "Honey, there is nothing you can do to stop me from loving you! Whatever it is, it's okay!" Dropping her head, she told me she aborted a pregnancy at age 16. I could see the hopelessness, the despair, the pain, the condemnation. She told me every time she looked at the two beautiful and miraculous little girls the Lord had given her, she felt unworthy. "You are my daughter, my youngest, my baby! There is nothing you can do to stop my love for you," I said! Holding her close, I told her the only person she needed to confess and repent to was Jesus. I reminded her that the sin was forgiven and forgotten. Emily assured me she repented, but it was clear she had not forgiven herself. By confessing to me, we both thought it was the release she needed to move forward and heal.

Never speaking of it again, I dismissed the abortion and never placed judgement on her. I discovered shortly after her death that she never found the healing she so desperately wanted and needed to move forward. According to her close friends, it was a topic she continued bringing up and the pain remained in her life. There was no closure, no healing. Emily carried the cloak of shame and condemnation, all lies from the enemy, to her death. God had a perfect plan, and it was not to die at the hands of the enemy...

> *For I know the thoughts that I think toward you, says the LORD, thoughts of peace and not of evil, to give you a future and a hope. Jeremiah 29:11 (NKJV)*

Looking back at my journal entries, this is one I wrote while struggling to understand the depths of my daughter's pain (date unknown)...

> *If we do not fully surrender ourselves to God, we are always looking over our shoulders to see what or who might satisfy us, help us, love us, or give us. We are unfaithful in our hearts toward God, the one Who will never leave us, disappoint us, or fail to love us. We are unable to feel His love if we are not living as He intended. As long as we remain unbroken and unsubmitted to God, we are looking to sources other than God to meet our needs.*
>
> *SELF CONDEMNATION stunts a relationship with Jesus by keeping us from interactions with Him. Instead of enjoying the peace of God, those who are trapped by*

shame often fear His rejection and feel driven to prove their worth. Instead of saying I am wrong, they say I am bad! Some people stubbornly attempt to live the Christian life in their own strength. That kind of life is marked by discontent. Peace will be fleeting, and loneliness will feel like the heart's permanent resident!

Taking a journey into Emily's pain was part of my healing. It was unavoidable if I had any hope of comprehending how she could take her own life. In one of the books given to me was a chapter named, *"The Cup Analogy."* Imagine if you will, a cup of water sitting on a table. It is so full it is rounded at the top. One or two drops of water are added to the cup and it spills over. What caused the water to spill? We want to blame the last one or two drops, but in an empty cup it would not spill. It was not the water in the cup prior to the drops being added, because if left alone, it would not have spilled. It was a combination of all the drops of water in the cup that came before and the last one or two drops that caused the water to spill. In a person's life, the water in the cup is symbolic of all the hurt, pain, shame, humiliation, and loss not dealt with along the way. The last couple of drops symbolize the "trigger events," "the last straw," the event or situation that preceded the final act of taking one's own life. Often we want to blame the trigger event, but this does not make sense to us. Like the water, these events alone would not cause someone to end their life. It is the combination of everything in that person's life not dealt with; the last one or two things that cause our loved ones to lose hope.

For survivors, we must find a way to pour out the water along the way. We must learn to deal with our pain in a way our loved ones could not. This analogy does not give us the concrete answer many of us are looking for, but I know it made sense and has been helpful for me. It allowed me to end the search for why, and who I should blame.

Emily's abortion was not the only drop of pain in her cup, but it consumed the majority of the cup...like one big drop...bigger than all the rest. It was the drop the enemy used to oppress her with the lies of shame, condemnation, and unworthiness. I am only guessing, but I believe satan told her that God could never love her the same. <u>Receiving God's love, and knowing the extent of His love, is how we conquer the enemy!</u>

Emily first belonged to God and was ours only for a while. She left two precious gifts...Ryleigh and Sadie. Thank you, God! In all things, I give thanks! I pray daily for Ryleigh and Sadie to be happy, healthy, to seek and love the Lord, and to never forget their mother's love for them. I pray that they will grow to have her same tender spirit and heart and have compassion for others as she did. When she didn't have it to give, she would share what little she had with those less fortunate. That compassion began at a young age. One afternoon, she overheard Andy and me talking about finances, grabbed her piggy bank, and tried to give it to us. "Will this help," she asked? As an adult, Emily purchased a used washer and dryer from a needy single mother. She said to me, "Mom, I saw this woman's living condition and I realized how blessed I am. I had an extra $20 and I knew she needed it more!"

A prayer for you…

"Dear Lord, I lift up your grieving sons and daughters, those whom are asking the 'why' questions! As they cry out to you, Lord, I am confident that You will provide laborers, scriptures, songs, and even creation to provide the answers they so desperately need! Provide comfort, Father, in this hour of desperation. In Jesus' name, A-men"

Scriptures: Psalm 20, Jeremiah 33:3, Psalm 17:6, Psalm 38:15, Psalm 86:7, Isaiah 30:19

Chapter Four

Stepping into The Light

Five years later, December 2, 2020, I know I must complete this writing as my grief journey has taken me to higher ground, and more of the Lord and His Word has been revealed to me. It is no coincidence that my sister, Karen, reached out to ask me for a copy of my previous memoir. It is 10:30 in the morning, and I have been reflecting on it for several hours since she contacted me. Reading it again, after several years, brought a renewed revelation on just how far I have traveled with the Lord. On December 2, 2015 (date of original writing), my pain was extreme, but even in the pain the Lord was preparing me for something bigger. I was in the beginning stages of the Lord revealing His truth, taking me from milk to meat, religion to relationship, beauty for ashes, and joy after mourning.

I began to reflect on the story of Deuteronomy 29:29 in my mother's life. Holy Spirit led me to the Bible to read and study this scripture again. I immediately noticed that in my original writing, I never completed the verse. I stopped at...*the secret things belong to the Lord.* This has so much to say about the condition of my relationship with the Lord, and my knowledge of Him during that season of my life. I will now finish this verse...

The secret things belong to the LORD our God, but those things which are revealed belong to us and to our children forever, that we may do all the words of this law. Deuteronomy 29:29 (NKJV)

Thank you, Jesus, that this journey has been a continuation of many things you have revealed to me, and that my story and testimony is still unfolding!

I quickly discovered two areas that I have received revelation and truth since my original writing.

<u>Truth One</u>: It is not God's will for bad things to happen. Bad things are works of the enemy because we live in a fallen world...

The thief does not come except to steal, and to kill, and to destroy. I have come that they may have life, and

> *that they may have it more abundantly. John 10:10 (NKJV)*

<u>Truth Two</u>: I have power and authority over the enemy as I am equipped with the full armor of God as a Spirit-filled Christian found in the book of Luke and Ephesians…

> *Behold, I give you the authority to trample on serpents and scorpions, and over all the power of the enemy, and nothing shall by any means hurt you. Luke 10:19 (NKJV)*

> *10 Finally, my brethren, be strong in the Lord and in the power of His might. 11 Put on the whole armor of God, that you may be able to stand against the wiles of the devil. 12 For we do not wrestle against flesh and blood, but against principalities, against powers, against the rulers of the darkness of this age, against spiritual hosts of wickedness in the heavenly places. 13 Therefore, take up the whole armor of God, that you may be able to withstand in the evil day, and having done all, to stand. Ephesians 6:10-13 (NKJV)*

It is clear in my writing that I was in search of answers, and it was clear that I was not aware of satan's involvement. I will not capitalize the "s" in satan; he has been brought to nothing, in Jesus name! I was hearing from the Lord, and He began His work on me, but there was a literal choking process as I was moving from milk to meat. I was a product of Hosea 4:6…

> *My people are destroyed for lack of knowledge. Because you have rejected knowledge, I also will reject you from being priest for Me; because you have forgotten the law of your God, I also will forget your children. Hosea 4:6 (NKJV)*

This is not talking about school knowledge. This refers to lack of knowing God's Word. His Word is His will.

At the time of my tragedy, I was a Christian, but had no power. I only had the faith for my ticket to Heaven. I was raised in a church that preached the cross, salvation, and the consequences of satan's burning hell with an eternity of torture and gnashing of teeth. All truth, and I am thankful for that church and the grandmother who picked me up in her blue Chevy at the end of my long driveway every Sunday, but I never heard sermons on what I should do after my salvation, or about who I was in Christ.

I Did Not Know

I DID NOT KNOW the book of Acts, the power of the Holy Spirit falling <u>upon</u> Christ's followers, and what really happened on the day of Pentecost.

I DID NOT KNOW that the book of Acts continues today, and that the supernatural encounters never had an expiration date!

I DID NOT KNOW that I was commanded to go out into the world and do the same thing as the disciples, the Great Commission to *ALL* who believe...

> *14 Later He appeared to the eleven as they sat at the table; and He rebuked their unbelief and hardness of heart, because they did not believe those who had seen Him after He had risen. 15 And He said to them, "Go into all the world and preach the gospel to every creature. 16 He who believes and is baptized will be saved; but he who does not believe will be condemned. 17 And these signs will follow those who believe: In My name they will cast out demons; they will speak with new tongues; 18 they will take up serpents; and if they drink anything deadly, it will by no means hurt them; they will lay hands on the sick, and they will recover." Mark 16:14-20 (NKJV)*

As far as I was concerned, everything was for the twelve disciples, and ended with the twelve. I had my ticket to Heaven, but everything that happened here on earth was God's will, good or bad, and I was to accept it and wait for joy in heaven. I often referred to this wrongful thinking as a box of chocolates, *you never know what you are going to get.*

I DID NOT KNOW that my words contained power, and they were a weapon that would be for me, or against me…

Death and life are in the power of the tongue, and those who love it will eat its fruit. Proverbs 18:21 (NKJV)

I DID NOT KNOW I had angels assigned to me, and that my words, when aligned with God's words, increased their strength and harkened them to minster to me. I envisioned angels as cute, little, cherub looking beings with golden hair sitting on clouds and playing their harps!

Are they not all ministering spirits sent forth to minister for those who will inherit salvation? Hebrews 1:14 (NKJV)

Bless the Lord, you His angels, who excel in strength, who do His word, heeding the voice of His word. Psalm 103:20 (NKJV)

Giving Place to the Devil

God had been placed on a shelf and was saved for emergencies only. I had opened every door and window to the enemy, and so had the rest of my family, including my daughter, Emily. We lived dangerously every day in enemy territory. God never moved…we did. We were not committing serious crimes or sins that were apparent to us, yet everything about our lives was filled with sin. There was lack of trust, lack of faith, fear, worry, bitterness, and even idolatry. The devil roams around like a roaring lion, looking for someone whom he MAY devour…

Be sober, be vigilant; because your adversary, the devil, walks about like a roaring lion, seeking whom he <u>may</u> devour. 1 Peter 5:8 (NKJV)

We had given the enemy legal right to devour us. We fell into the group of Christians…*whom he <u>may</u> devour.* The old me would think that scripture was for the lost person. No, Peter was writing to Christians. It is a message of warning to Christ followers.

One of the most misguided Biblical teachings I heard growing up, and even in my adult life, was found in 1 Corinthians. If I am going to be honest, I need to say that it could have destroyed my life.

> *No temptation has overtaken you except such as is common to man; but God is faithful, who will not allow you to be tempted beyond what you are able, but with the temptation will also make the way of escape, that you may be able to bear it. 1 Corinthians 10:13 (NKJV)*

I can still hear my granny say, when attempting to quote that scripture, "The Lord will not put more on you than you can bear!" Never once, did I look up that scripture and read it for myself. It was spoken from the pulpit, and from my family, so that was all I needed to hear. In my mind, it was God's fault and His will if anything bad happened in my life!

I was beginning to see how scriptures could be taken out of context, especially if you had no knowledge of the book's purpose, the author, the audience, and the culture of that day. One morning in my quiet time with the Lord, He directed me to 1 Corinthians 10:13. I read all of chapter 10, now with a newfound understanding. The key word in this scripture is "temptation." Temptation does not come from God (Hebrews 2:18). God never tempts us. This may come as a shock to many people, but God does not trick, tempt, or give us opportunities to sin. This is contrary to His nature. Jesus underwent this type of temptation and testing so we would not have to. After all, the Bible records that Jesus was led by the Spirit into the desert to be tempted and tested by the devil (Matthew 4:1, Mark 1:12-13, Luke 4:1-2). In this testing, Jesus proved His faithfulness both to God and mankind. Since this was a victory, we will never be tempted by God. James makes this very clear...

When tempted, no one should say, "God is tempting me, for God cannot be tempted by evil, nor does He tempt anyone." James 1:13 (NKJV)

When the ENEMY tempts you (some translations use the word test), God is faithful and will not allow you to be tempted beyond what you are able, because HE WILL PROVIDE AN ESCAPE, A WAY OUT! I found it interesting that I never heard the last part of that scripture when quoted...the part where God will *provide an escape*!! If God is the one tempting me, why would He provide an escape, or a way out? This scripture is a beautiful promise of how God will deliver His children (same as the Israelites, same as common to man) from the enemy, yet

He is blamed for the works of the enemy on many occasions. I cannot tell you the freedom I received when the Lord revealed the truth about this scripture! At that moment, I knew my mind had to be renewed from thinking and saying that everything in my life was God's will! At that moment, the enemy had been caught!

I had a personal encounter during my journey where this *provision of escape* was put into place. Almost on a silver platter! Did I see it? The answer is no! The first problem was my lack of knowing the Word (Hosea 4:6). Secondly, I was so full of anger and bitterness my eyes could not see, nor my ears hear, that a way out was being provided. I was blocked from receiving my escape because I had given place to the devil! Ephesians 4:26-27 warns us about this…"Be angry, and do not sin, do not let the sun go down on your wrath, nor give place to the devil."

A prayer for you…

"Heavenly Father, may the reader of this book have full knowledge of Your Word. May they desire to read with their own eyes, and never allow misguided truths to sink into their minds and hearts. Meet them there, Lord, as you did me. May they know who the real enemy is, and may they hear you on every page. Whatever they are going through, I pray they will catch the enemy and place him underneath their feet. If salvation is needed, I ask for their heart to be softened and their face turn to You! My desire is for every reader to know You, trust You, and surrender everything to You. You are their Father, their deliverer, their defender, their counselor, their helper, their teacher…You are their Healer, King of Kings, Lord of Lords, Yeshua, Alpha and Omega, Master, Savior! There is no name above the name of Jesus! Victory is for this reader, in Jesus' name! Hallelujah! A-men"

Scriptures: John 3:16, Hosea 4:6, Romans 12:2, John 10:10, Luke 10:19, Psalm 139, Psalm 23

Scriptures for salvation: Romans 3:23, Romans 6:23, Romans 5:8, Romans 2:4, Romans 10:9, Romans 10:13

Chapter Five
Psalm 91

In August of 2016, fifteen months after Emily's death, I experienced a supernatural encounter in my prayer room. I was in the middle of a court battle that was related to Emily's death. This case should have taken approximately three months, but it was still not final fifteen months later. Once again…crying out to the only One who could deliver me! King Jesus! Crying out in desperation, I felt a strong desire to pick up my Bible. I opened it, not really knowing where I would go after I did, and the first place it opened was Psalm 91. I only had a few scriptures hidden away in my heart, and Psalm 91 was not one of them. It had a title that read, *God, my Defender*. Even at the glance of the title, I knew this was not a coincidence. I read it out loud, not knowing at that time the power of the spoken

Word...rhema! What is rhema? It literally means an "utterance" or "thing said." It is a specific Word from the Lord that applies to us individually...a *spoken* Word.

I heard my voice, of course, as I read the verses out loud, but then something happened. The supernatural! Although I could hear myself, it was as if another took over. I felt chains fall off my body; chains of anger, bitterness, fear, and defeat. Without fully understanding at the time, I was baptized in the Holy Spirit! I had a filling! An overflowing! I received power from on high...

> *Behold, I send the Promise of My Father upon you; but tarry in the city of Jerusalem until you are endued with power from on high." Luke 24:49 (NKJV)*

Still reading, I had a vision. I saw a courtroom in Heaven, and I heard the Lord say, "I am your attorney, I am free of charge, I am your defender, I am the Most High God and this court is the Most High Court, there is none higher, surrender, and give this case to Me, and you will receive your breakthrough!" I am tingling all over right now just reliving this moment in writing! What a Holy Ghost encounter! As I am reflecting on this encounter, and what amazes me the most, I did not know anything about a courtroom in Heaven, or that one existed (I recommend reading the book, *Operating in the Courts of*

Heaven, by Robert Henderson). I felt like a little girl with Daddy holding me in His lap, telling me, *I Got This*! Only this time, I believed it! With full surrender on my part, the Lord was able to go to work on my behalf...

> *Beloved, do not avenge yourselves, but rather give place to wrath; for it is written, "Vengeance is Mine, I will repay," says the Lord. Romans 12:19 (NKJV)*

With Andy coming into quick agreement, I called our attorney and ended the court case. We literally signed the papers to surrender; waving the white flag. I never felt so free! God is faithful, and He cannot lie. Within 30 days, I received my breakthrough!

Soar High on Wings Like Eagles

When the chains fell off during my Psalm 91 encounter, and with the filling of Holy Spirit, I could now use both wings to soar. I had a literal feeling of flying...soaring. I was on the eagle, being lifted high above the earth...looking below at my adversaries. It is best described in Isaiah 40:31...*But they who wait for the LORD shall renew their strength; they shall mount up with wings like eagles; they shall run and not be weary; they shall walk and not faint.*

A bird must use both wings to fly, to soar, to lift above and flee from their enemies. Have you ever seen a bird with a broken wing? There is an enormous effort to fly but it cannot because there is only one good wing. I want to use the *"one wing"* analogy to describe the importance of both <u>trust</u> and <u>surrender</u>. You will never soar above your enemy if you only trust. For months, I walked around confessing that I trusted the Lord. I read the Word and said, "I trust You, Lord! I do, I do, I do!" The fact of the matter is, I continued to take matters into my own hands with the physical act of making things happen…the legal battle! It was physical, tangible, something I could see, touch, and feel; something I could control. Sound familiar in your life? In my mind, it was a must! However, "I trust you, Lord," I said!

Only upon fully surrendering, releasing my control, using the other wing, could I spread both wings and fly. Wing of trust; wing of surrender!

Do you have a broken wing? Like me, do you confess over and over that you trust the Lord, yet only continue taking control? Ask the Lord, He will reveal it to you.

Walking in Peace

One morning, shortly after the Psalm 91 encounter, I was praying and thanking God for our journey together, and for all He was doing in my life. I was still grieving, and still struggling with the pain associated with it. In this prayer, I remember saying that I knew I would enjoy life again and would one day see light at the end of the storm. When I opened my eyes, they immediately fell on the white, bright, streaks in the painting of Jesus carrying me...

I felt my spirit leap! I knew at that moment it was significant, yet I did not fully understand. What I didn't know was that I had painted my first painting while being led by the Holy Spirit, in December of 2015, during the darkest part of my grief journey. It was the beginning of the plan and purpose God had waiting for me. The Lord quickly led me to the book of John. Now my painting had scripture to go with it! Thank you, Jesus, for bringing me out of darkness...

And the light shines in the darkness, and the darkness did not comprehend it. John 1:5 (NKJV)

A prayer for you...

"Father, Your Word says you are not a respecter of persons, so do it again, Lord! Same as me, may this reader have an encounter with You that lifts them to an unexplainable place of rest and peace! Thank You, Lord, for Psalm 91. Thank You, Lord, for the power of Your rhema Word; the spoken Word! Pour out Your Spirit on the brokenhearted and the grieving, in Jesus' name! A-men!"

Scriptures: Psalm 91, Acts 10:34, Mark 8:34-37, John 14:21, Matthew 10:29-31, Isaiah 49:15

Chapter Six

New Beginnings

Things were happening very quickly in the third year of my journey, the year of 2018. I was now a Spirit-filled Christian growing in faith. I knew what real peace felt like after my Psalm 91 encounter, so it was easy to identify circumstances in my life that were not in alignment with God's will. I was still selling real estate for a well-known Atlanta builder, and managing new homes communities. This was a career I thought I would retire from with over twenty years and counting. I was extremely successful, with a consistent six figure salary. This career had become my identity. Every discussion I had with family and friends revolved around who I was in the work force. Working almost seven days a week, including every weekend, I felt like

I was a possession rather than a person. There was also a feeling of being trapped because of the future income outside of my reach, like a dangling carrot. Most contracts were six months in the building process, and my pay was not calculated until after closing. Money was always on the table, so I had to stay, keep going, and keep selling in order to receive what I had worked very hard for. It was a cycle that seemed impossible to break. During my commutes to the sales office, I remember having feelings of anxiety. I was also having strange encounters on many of those mornings. Bright, red, cardinals would fly directly in front of my car, from one side of the street to the other, flying very low. It would always bring me back to the red cardinal encounter I had on the day of Emily's death. I often wondered what this meant…if anything. I was choking inside, but I did not feel like there was anything I could do. My workplace was an environment of foul language and back-stabbing. I knew in my spirit that I needed to remove myself if I wanted to continue my journey with the Lord.

In my prayer time one morning, the Lord led me to scripture in the book of II Chronicles that read…

> "But you, be strong and do not let your hands be weak, for your work shall be rewarded." II Chronicles 15:7 (NKJV)

There it was again, another quickening in my spirit! I knew that I was the *"you"* in this verse, and the Lord was speaking directly to me! Still never imagining myself leaving real estate, I tried to mold and manipulate this scripture into my current job and career. For three months, I prayed and meditated on this scripture, never once thinking about the gift of art the Lord had given me, but knowing deep down that another shift in my life was coming.

Learning to Trust God

After a few more months had passed, I began to realize that the Lord was telling me to end my real estate career and trust Him with the next step. I was hearing in my spirt, *I created you to paint.* In obedience, I turned in my notice and walked away from a career that held me in chains. I didn't know how I was going to replace the income we had so grown accustomed to, or what was going to happen next, but after the supernatural breakthrough I had already experienced I was not about to start doubting the Lord now! Finally, there was complete peace and joy in my life! I was trusting God with all matters that concerned me, and my prayers transitioned from begging to confessing His promises. I was able to remember the good times I had with Emily and her children, and turn my focus away from the pain of her death that kept me in the grips of grief.

I reached out to family and friends and announced that I would be painting again, only this time for hire. I painted pets, happy places, and landscapes. Making $13,000 my first year as a middle-aged artist, the enemy started telling me I would be another starving artist. Lord, where are we going with this?

Another shift came, or maybe I should say a new level. I had this inner desire, not realizing it was from the Lord, to paint a lion. After it was completed, I heard in my spirit that it was supposed to hang in the new church that Andy and I were now partnering with, *Christ Fellowship Church* in Dawsonville, Georgia. We were drawn to the North Georgia Revival that began in February 2018, which was all part of God's plan. When I presented the lion painting to Pastors Todd and Karen and told them about my prompting, Pastor Karen spoke a word over me that neither of us knew at the time carried an anointing or was prophetic. She said to me, "Joanne, you need to paint on stage." I remember thinking, is she nuts? It took me hours to paint this lion, so how in the world would I sit on stage and pull something like this off! I almost laughed at Pastor Karen with thoughts of…*bless her heart, she has no clue!* Little did I know! Following that word, I had two other people speak something similar during casual conversation. In both, the words flew right over my head…my ears could not hear! Thank you, Jesus, for not giving up on me! Thank you, Jesus, for continuing to send laborers to speak until my ears heard!

Painting with Jesus

On March 19, 2019, I finally heard! I received a prophetic Word that I would be painting in the Spirit during worship and praise. It was spoken that these paintings would bring healing and deliverance. It was spoken that I would teach women and children, especially children, how to finger paint with the Lord. My mind and emotions were spinning as I was trying to receive and understand this Word! I did not know what painting in the Sprit meant, or how it worked, until diving deeper. For four solid weeks I wrestled with the Lord, trying to understand prophetic painting. My house was filled with paints of all colors, canvases of all sizes, and easels on the floor and tables. Brushes in both hands, I was waiting for fire to fall from Heaven and miraculously take control. "Please Lord, PLEASE!" Begging for a miracle, I attempted to paint every angel and heavenly scene from my flesh, most of which ended up in the trash. I was convinced I was not the one.

On May 7, 2019, I was asked to paint for the first time. As I approached the stage, with sweaty palms and trembling hands, I looked at the blank canvas and painted a large green 3 with a key hanging on the bottom. It was a vision the Lord gave me the night before as I was asking Him to give me a clue ahead of time. "Lord, please don't send me up there in front of all those people with nothing to paint," I cried! After the painting was finished, the preacher approached me and said,

"Do you have any idea what you've painted?"

"Please tell me," I asked!

He said, "You have just prophetically painted a symbol for this season we are entering…the Lord is unlocking the Third Great Awakening and the color green represents restoration and prosperity."

These paintings are speaking into people's lives just as it was prophesied. Although I know more is coming, I have started to impart into young people and children by holding prophetic art classes. I see each week how the children are drawn to the paintings, and some are even speaking over them or revealing what they see.

Journal Entry – December 20, 2020

The Night "Macie Love" painted in the Spirit

On December 20, 2020, during the morning worship and praise service, I had a vision of a second easel and canvas to the left of mine, only smaller. I knew it was in preparation for a child. I felt the urgency that it was to be for the revival service that night, week 150. While dealing with thoughts of how I was going to make that second set up work, I then realized this second person would be a little girl. I asked, "Lord, if this is all You, where will I find this little girl so quickly, and how will I get a second set up within the next several hours?" I heard in my spirit...*don't fret, I'll send her to you, you will know.* As for the additional set up, I knew that Andy could do it. I had a second easel at home and all I had to do was ask. He is the one who makes things happen for me on stage.

Before Pastor Todd preached, he brought out a family to give their testimonies from their baptism the week before. Wes and Kelly Lammey, and their daughter Macie. As I am looking at Macie standing on stage, realizing she was the first *little girl* my eyes fixed upon since my vision, I immediately asked the Lord, "Is that her, Lord?" I just needed a sign...something...don't leave me hanging now! One by one, this family gave their testimony. When Pastor Todd asked Macie, age seven, what happened to her in the water, she said she went to Heaven and saw Jesus, her grandmother, and her brother who was now big (he died at birth). Macie said that Heaven was *crazy beautiful*! After hearing this, I knew Macie was the one! I knew she would be painting scenes of Heaven with all the amazing colors! My heart began to pound because I knew I had to tell Pastor Karen, which meant getting up and going over to her while Pastor Todd was still speaking with this family. Holding back as long as I could, I finally felt as if I was being pushed out of my chair! We give God the keys to the house, so staying in your seat is not always what He has on the agenda! I moved as quietly as I could over to Pastor Karen and shared everything with her up to that moment, then returned to my seat. Not knowing this would happen, I was called up on the stage to share my vision. Needless to say, I was blown away at what was taking place and without a doubt felt the presence of the Holy Ghost!

After the service, I connected with Macie and her parents to talk about my vision. I told Macie what I had seen, and I asked her if she wanted to paint with me and Jesus on stage that night. There was no fear! It is almost as if she knew, and of course she said, "yes!" I told her that Jesus would tell her what to paint, and I never shared with her what I felt in my spirit to paint.

My painting: I saw my heart floating in the atmosphere transmitting to Heaven's frequencies, as I was dialing in to hear the Lord's voice. This is how I felt during my vision with thoughts of doubt, *Lord is this You, or are they my thoughts*? As I dialed in, the Lord breathed on me!

Macie's painting: She painted a blue sky with layers of colorful hearts, used her fingers to put dots all inside and around the hearts, then surrounded them by a white circular ring. She shared with me afterwards that the blue sky in heaven is beautiful!

You can't make this stuff up...

#1) We both painted hearts! Macie's mom, Kelly, told me that Macie shared with her what she was going to paint prior to the service...a heart! I never communicated to Macie, or anyone, what the Lord had given me to paint.

#2) The Sunday night prior (week 149, December 13th), Macie was seen in the hallway touching all my paintings before her baptism, one by one, then went to the art table and picked up one of my cards as a souvenir. Her dad, Wes, told me that she loved the paintings so much he had to bribe her with buying one of them so she would stay for the adult service, knowing they would be giving their testimony instead of going to the kid's service. I did not know about any of this until the night of December 20th!

#3) During the Sunday morning service on December 20th, Pastor Todd spoke about how God's timing and the body of Christ were coming together...like connecting the dots (the game we used to play). There are dots on both paintings, and as I looked at them the Lord reminded me what he spoke, what he released into the spiritual realm, setting the stage for both paintings...connecting the dots; connecting the two families!

#4) The date, December 20, 2020! After Macie and I finished painting, and during the service, I kept thinking about the date. I knew it was significant, but I did not know the meaning. We know that dates and numbers are extremely significant as the Bible gives us a perfect example of this. Because the Lord is so good, and He knew my heart's desire was to know about this date, He sent Hannah Fowler over to me. She said, "I think we need to look up the meaning of number 20." I immediately thought...*GET READY, HERE IT COMES!* **Number 20 in Bible symbolizes the cycles of completeness. It is not so widely used, but often it is connected to a perfect period of waiting, labor or suffering that is compared to a trial and rewarded**. The dots in the paintings were **connecting** us together! Both families have lived through **cycles**, walked through a long journey of **waiting**, experiencing **trials, pain, and suffering**, and praise God we will see the **rewards** here and now as our testimonies will shout across the land.

#5) As I was painting the breath of God, He was breathing on Macie. It was even pointing toward her, and above her!

#6) Before the night ended, Macie gave me her painting and I gave her mine. I wrote a message to her on the back of my painting, the one I gave to her, and while doing that I asked how she spelled her name. Now I learned that her middle name is *Love*! Not a nick name, but her actual birth given middle name! We had just painted hearts, and it is LOVE that breaks all chains! The Word tells us that we can have all the gifts from Heaven...but without love, we have nothing.

> *"And though I have the gift of prophecy, and understand all mysteries and all knowledge, and though I have all faith, so that I could remove mountains, but have not love, I am nothing."* 1 Corinthians 13:2
> (NKJV)

Taylor Bahin

Taylor is a beautiful, young woman in her mid-twenties. She and her family attend our church at Christ Fellowship, and are involved with the North Georgia Revival. Her father, Joseph, would often come to my art table before and after services to tell me about her amazing artistic ability, but then his story would take a turn and I could see pain in his face when he described how dark and demonic her art had turned. He would say, "I know that God has created her to paint for Him, I want her to come by your table to see your art; if only she would come hang out with you." I could feel his pain, and on one occasion we prayed together...confessing that Taylor would fall in love with Jesus, and her art would take a drastic turn to beauty and light.

Several months later, Andy received a phone call from Joseph. "Andy, I need for you and Joanne to start praying right now! Taylor is having suicidal thoughts and we are heading to the church now to see Pastor Todd," cried Joseph! Andy came to me immediately, and we both got down on our knees, held hands, and rebuked the spirit of suicide on Taylor's life! We confessed what the Word says about Taylor, "Lord, it is not Your will for Taylor to be depressed, oppressed, and desiring to take her life…this is the work of the enemy and we bind him, in Jesus name! Your will is for Taylor to live and not die, in Jesus name!"

Several hours after we prayed, and anxiously waiting on a word from Joseph, we received his call. He proceeds to tell us that Pastor Todd got into the baptismal waters with Taylor…the place where Jesus had met thousands from all around the world! The place where thousands had been set free from sickness, pain, addictions, and suicidal thoughts! Taylor cried out to Jesus, was baptized, filled with the Holy Spirit, and came up out of the water singing in her new prayer language! The bondage and chains from the enemy fell off and died in the water!

While under the water, Taylor sees a bright, blue, flame shaped like a cross. Blue is the hottest flame, the purest flame! Her desire to paint darkness was instantly transformed into a desire to paint light...the light of Christ! Below is a black and white picture of her first prophetic painting! The original painting has brilliant shades of blue, depicting Taylor's Holy Ghost encounter! She named it, *The Purest Light*.

Joseph's prayers have been answered as he now gets to watch his daughter, Taylor, join me at the art table and share in painting prophetically during services.

Sevenfold Recompense

The Word tells us when a thief (the enemy) is caught, he must pay back sevenfold. You seldom hear teachings on this, but there are many you will find with the proper search.

Yet when he is found, he must restore sevenfold; He shall give up all the substance of his house. Proverbs 6:31 (NKJV)

I have caught the enemy in so many areas of my life! He stole my childhood! He stole my identity! He stole my joy! He stole my daughter's life and robbed her children of their mother! Satan, I have caught you and now you must pay back! So how does that work? Can the Lord roll back the clock? He can do anything, and I have faith for miracles, so while I wait for more to be revealed He is showing me many areas where I am receiving a recompense beyond my wildest imagination!

After Emily's death, I feared her life would be forgotten! I cried out to Jesus on many occasions, and for many hours, asking

Him to never allow her life and death to go wasted...never realizing I would be the vessel used to answer that prayer! My testimony, the prophetic paintings, Macie Lemmey, Taylor Bahin, this book, and many others I have ministered to, are all part of my sevenfold recompense!

If you are scratching your head and trying to figure out how that would be considered as recompense from the enemy, let me explain in greater detail. For every painting that comes from my spirit, led by Holy Spirit, it is speaking to someone else. It brings healing, deliverance, and many times is used as confirmation for what that person is hearing from the Lord. That is a victory (soul) that the enemy lost! He did not see it coming...part of my sevenfold recompense! Hallelujah!

The Lord is using my prophetic paintings in this revival season to inspire, encourage, and prompt other young children to walk in their calling! Early in this season, the Lord revealed to me that He was raising up an army of artists! I see it happening right now at the North Georgia Revival. Children will gather around the stage just below where I am painting. They will watch! Some will be sketching and drawing on the floor during worship and praise! The enemy did not see it coming...sevenfold recompense! Hallelujah!

Taking it a little bit deeper, the Lord is showing me how He is restoring my childhood. How can that be?? When I paint in the Spirit, especially when I am using my hands and being prompted and moved by the worship and praise, I feel as if I am a child again…finger painting with Jesus! It is as though we are the only two on the stage! Just me and Jesus! There is a peace and joy I cannot explain. The enemy did not see it coming…part of my sevenfold recompense! Hallelujah!

The act of painting, and the love of art itself has been restored! The Lord created me to paint, and the enemy stole it early in my life. As a young child, I remember how I would paint when troubled or afraid. No one in my family told me it was a gift from God, or a calling from Him. My mother would say, "No one in our family has this talent, I wonder where you got it?" I was always searching for a family member from whom I had inherited the talent. No one ever surfaced!

I painted and gave away…painted and gave away. I never kept any of my work! My paintings were never originals because I would always look at something that inspired me, usually something from a magazine (no internet back in those days). I would cut out the image from the magazine and copy it. Detail by detail. My favorite paintings were of flowers and landscapes, and my medium was oil. I loved the smell of oil paints, especially the linseed oil and turpentine used for thinning and cleaning.

Because I copied another artist's painting, or used a photo, I heard in my spirit that I was cheating. "A copycat," was what I labeled myself. For this reason, I NEVER allowed anyone to call me an artist. The enemy was whispering in my ear..."you are not an artist, you are not an artist, you are not an artist!" I believed that lie, then another lie that said I could never make any money selling my "copycat" art. After high school, I dropped the painting all together and sought out a world's career to sustain me throughout life.

Today, I call myself an artist! I say it because I believe it! There is power in knowing who you are in Christ! There is freedom in knowing that I am a daughter of the Most-High King! The enemy did not see it coming...sevenfold recompense! Hallelujah!

A prayer for you…

*"Lord Jesus, may we never forget that through our adversities we will find rest in Your Word. You are a God of restoration! Thank You, Jesus! Restore health and heal our wounds as promised in Jeremiah 30:17! Lord, may we believe right now that Your Word has the final say, and restoration is Your will! As King David proclaimed, may we also proclaim and acknowledge that **we believe** in order to see the goodness of God in the land of the living! Father, we acknowledge that You are for us, in Jesus' name! A-men!"*

Scriptures: Jeremiah 30:17, Psalm 27:13, Romans 8:31, Joel 2:21-26, Psalm 51:12, Nehemiah 8:10, Proverbs 6:30-31, Isaiah 61:7

Chapter Seven
I Have Overcome

"And they overcame him by the blood of the Lamb and by the word of their testimony, and they did not love their lives to the death."
Revelation 12:11 (NKJV)

My testimony is being lived out through Romans 8:28…what the enemy meant for bad, the Lord will turn around for good when we seek His face. The enemy did not see my act of obedience and testimony coming! By crying out to Jesus in my pain and seeking His face and His will for my life, the enemy's plan to destroy me was cancelled. I closed all the windows and doors that were once open to him!

On the day of Emily's celebration of life service, just seven days after her death, I had my first vision. In this vision it was dark, but I saw myself on a platform. I knew I was raised up above others who were off in the distance, and that I was doing something significant, but could not see what it was. I also realized there were hundreds, maybe thousands, watching me. Unless there is more to this vision yet to be revealed, I have arrived! I paint every Sunday night on stage during worship and praise at the *North Georgia Revival* in my hometown of Dawsonville, Georgia. The date February 11, 2021, marked three years of this revival. People from all over the world are coming each week to receive a touch from the Lord. It is also aired live around the world through the *ISN network*!

In addition to painting in the Spirit during worship and praise, I minister globally through my website at *inspirationsbyjo.com*. I also travel and give my testimony when and where the Lord leads. I have overcome the enemy!

It has been six years since my daughter's death, and not a day goes by that I do not think about her. Her daughters, Ryleigh and Sadie, are still living apart and visit three to four times a year together with me and the rest of the family. I see them growing up quickly in a world that is darker than the previous generation. I cover them with prayers of intercession and declaration; calling forth things that are not, as though they are (Romans 4:17).

I am now at peace, which allows me to focus on the testimony and ministry that God has entrusted to me. I know we are living in the end days; the *Third Great Awakening*! All the earth will be covered by His glory as there are pockets of revival breaking out all over the globe! I know Emily is in Heaven waiting for the rest of us. For every day I wait, is another day I am closer to seeing her again.

A prayer for you…

"Father, I ask for peace and rest to come quickly to the grieving heart reading this book. May they seek Your face, and may they know that you are the only Comforter. Guide them to Your Word for knowledge and wisdom needed for their journey. May they seek blessings from brokenness, beauty for ashes, and joy from mourning. May their testimony be heard and used to defeat the enemy! These things I pray, in Jesus' name. Amen!"

Scriptures: Revelation 12:11, Psalm 63:1, Matthew 7:7, Psalm 34:4, Psalm 55:6, Isaiah 61:3, Matthew 11:28-29, Psalm 145

Receive Jesus as Your Savior

Choosing to receive Jesus Christ as your Lord and Savior is the most important decision you will ever make!

God's Word promises, "If you confess with your mouth the Lord Jesus and believe in your heart that God raised Him from the dead, you will be saved." (Romans 10:9 NKJV)

By His grace, God has already done everything to provide salvation, and your part is simply to believe and receive.

Pray this prayer out loud…

Lord Jesus, for too long I have kept you out of my life. I know that I am a sinner and that I cannot save myself. No longer will I close the door when I hear you knocking. By faith I gratefully receive your gift of salvation. I am ready to trust you as my Lord and Savior. Thank you, Lord Jesus, for coming to earth. I believe you are the Son of God who died on the cross for my sins and rose from the dead on the third day. Thank you for bearing my sins and giving me the gift of eternal life. I believe your Words are true. Come into my heart, Lord Jesus, and be my Savior. A-men.

Prophetic Paintings (book) has over 60 colored images, along with journal entries, from my first year of painting prophetically. Can be purchased through Amazon.

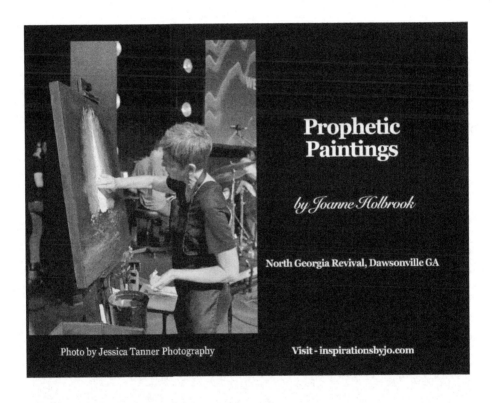

For more information about available original paintings, prints, stretched canvases, and other items with images from my paintings, visit my Art Store at www.inspirationsbyjo.com.

The Third Great Awakening

Painted May 7, 2019

Watch Out for the Children

Painted May 7, 2019

Fire on the Water

Painted July 28, 2019

On the Wings of an Eagle

Painted August 25, 2019

Spirit and Truth

Painted January 26, 2020

I Have Been Set Free

Painted January 18, 2020

The Lord Rules

Painted March 1, 2020

My Jesus

Painted June 16, 2020

Bride of Christ

Painted November 17, 2019

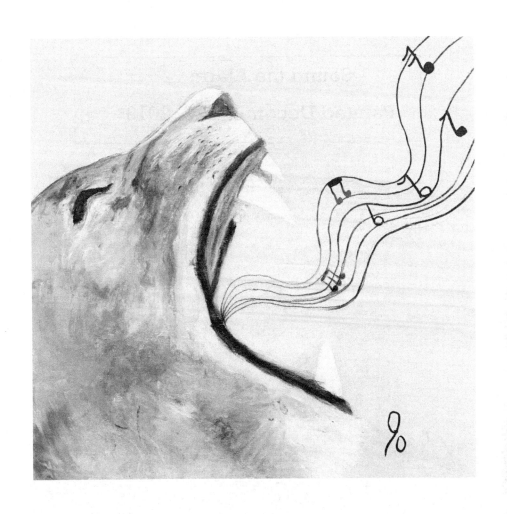

Singing Over Me

Painted January 19, 2020

Sound the Alarm
Painted December 22, 2019

I Am With You
Painted January 12, 2020

Sword of the Spirit
Painted November 10, 2019

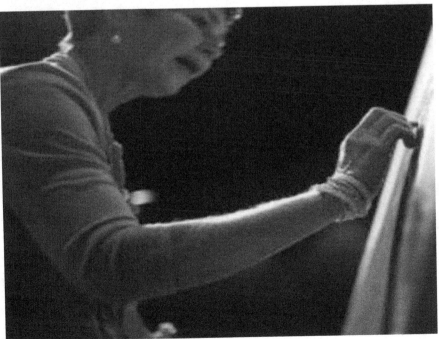

Made in the USA
Columbia, SC
07 June 2021